Original title:
Unrequited Feelings

Copyright © 2024 Swan Charm Publishing
All rights reserved.

Editor: Jessica Elisabeth Luik
Author: Eliora Lumiste
ISBN HARDBACK: 978-9916-86-084-7
ISBN PAPERBACK: 978-9916-86-085-4

Frail Yearnings

In twilight's tender glow, we stand
The dreams like whispers slip through hand
The time, relentless, draws its plan
The heart, it beats to understand

Beneath the moon's soft silver face
We search for moments, find no trace
In memory's depths, a fleeting grace
Of love's embrace, in time's own pace

The stars, they flicker far away
Their distant call, we wish to sway
Yet in their light, we cannot stay
For daybreak steals the night's array

With every breath, the shadows play
In silence, night and heart relay
For fragile hopes, we softly pray
That morn might keep the dark at bay

So let us hold what time bestows
In every tear, in every rose
For frail yearnings, their wisdom knows
Through fleeting days, the river flows

Lost Echoes

In hallways dim, where memories lie
The ghostly whispers, pass us by
Through empty rooms, the echoes sigh
Of times gone lost, beneath the sky

The faces fade, in shadows' shroud
Their voices soft, no longer loud
As silence falls, a heavy crowd
To dreams that once, our hearts had vowed

The years like waves, their tides erase
The footprints left, no lasting trace
Yet in the soul, a quiet place
Where echoes of the past embrace

In twilight hours, where shadows roam
The past returns, calls us back home
To moments lost, in silent poem
The heart's own lull, its gentle tome

So let us tread, where echoes drift
In every tear, a memory's gift
For in their loss, the spirits lift
To find within, the soul's true rift

Unheard Affection

In quiet corners love resides,
Unvoiced, unseen, yet it abides.
Behind closed lips, a silent prayer,
A hidden heart, a tender care.

In fleeting glances, whispers grow,
A silent bond, they barely show.
Through veils of silence, feelings steer,
Yet words unspoken, never hear.

The morning light, a gentle brush,
Touches hearts and fills the hush.
In shadows deep, affection lies,
A muted flame that never dies.

Withering Tears

Each tear falls, a crystal stream,
Echoes of a lost, sweet dream.
On cheeks they trace a silent trail,
Whispers of a heart's travail.

Through shadows dark, they softly flow,
Silent songs of silent woe.
In the dark, their stories blend,
A sorrowed tale that has no end.

But as the dawn brings light anew,
A wisp of hope appears in view.
Though tears may wither, hearts repair,
And find new strength, a love to share.

Hushed Reality

Beneath the surface, quietly,
Lives another reality.
Shadows dance and whispers play,
In the light of day's decay.

Unseen truths in silence bloom,
In the corners of a room.
Hushed are voices, thoughts adrift,
Bound by dreams and shadows' shift.

In nights so still, the secrets breathe,
Unraveled by the threads they weave.
Lives entwined in quiet plea,
A delicate hushed reality.

Fading Glances

Eyes that meet and then depart,
Brief encounters, fleeting start.
Moments caught in passing gleam,
Fading like a distant dream.

In the crowd, connections thin,
Silent notes on a violin.
A glance exchanged, then softly lost,
In the fabric time has tossed.

Yet in the dusk of memories,
Lives the spark of such brief ease.
Fading glances, tender ties,
Frozen moments in our eyes.

Invisible Touch

A whisper in the ether,
Soft fingers, cool embrace.
It lingers in its fleeting,
A ghost I cannot trace.

The air is filled with sighing,
An echo of a voice.
In silence, it entwines me,
Without a conscious choice.

This touch, it leaves me longing,
A brush that sparks a flame.
An unseen hand that guides me,
Through shadows, yet unnamed.

Ephemeral Desires

In moments barely captured,
Desires take their flight.
They rise like morning vapors,
Then fade into the night.

A glance, a brief connection,
A spark that's gone too fast.
These wishes, like the autumn,
Are never meant to last.

In dreams, they swirl like vapor,
Elusive as the breeze.
Ephemeral desires,
That bring me to my knees.

Shy Yearnings

In corners of the heart,
A timid wish resides.
Unspoken plea for love,
That hidden, gently hides.

It rises with the dawn,
Then softly drifts away.
These shy, unvoiced yearnings,
Afraid of light of day.

Yet in the quiet moments,
They whisper through the veil.
A silent, tender wish,
In pulses faint and frail.

Silent Craving

A hunger without voice,
A need without a name.
It echoes in the stillness,
A quiet, endless flame.

In shadows it will linger,
In silence it consumes.
This craving, deeply haunting,
It fills the empty rooms.

No words can quell this yearning,
No light can pierce its shroud.
A silent, endless craving,
That leaves the spirit bowed.

Secret Sorrows

In the shadows where echoes lie,
Silent whispers in the cold night sky.
Tears of ghosts that no one sees,
Hidden wounds beneath the trees.

Muffled cries in the dead of night,
Lonely hearts that shun the light.
Yearning voices speak in dreams,
Drowned in sorrow's silent streams.

Eyes that glisten with untold pain,
Veiled by clouds, like summer rain.
Burdened souls that time forgets,
Locked in chambers of regrets.

Eclipsed Affection

Beneath the stars, love fades to gray,
As shadows steal the light of day.
Hearts eclipsed by doubt and fear,
Love's sweet whispers disappear.

A tangled web of spoken lies,
Masks the truth in lovers' eyes.
Moonlight weaves a silent spell,
In the heart where shadows dwell.

Forgotten vows in twilight's haze,
Dreams adrift in endless maze.
Tender moments lost in time,
Echo faint like distant chime.

Invisible Cravings

Desires hidden, masked with care,
Secrets whispered to the air.
Fingers reaching towards the flame,
Yearning whispers call your name.

Silent wishes lost in mist,
Unspoken dreams through night persist.
Longing hearts with soulful gaze,
Seeking solace through the haze.

Unseen cravings linger near,
Lips that tremble with silent fear.
Eyes reflect the silent plea,
Boundless longing to be free.

Lost in Reverie

In the silence of the dawn,
Dreams of yesteryear are drawn.
Whispers from a distant shore,
Echoing forevermore.

Veils of time, a gentle weave,
Memories no longer cleave.
Drifting through a sea of dreams,
Nothing's truly as it seems.

Mind adrift in endless space,
Chased by shadows, time's embrace.
Wakened heart lost in despair,
Yearning for what isn't there.

The Mirror's Secret

Gaze within the glassy depth,
Seeking truth beyond the breath,
Shadows dance and whispers creep,
Mirrored secrets gently sleep.

Eyes reflect the lost desires,
Burning with forgotten fires,
In the whispers of the night,
Secrets drift in ghostly light.

Silvered surface holds the past,
Moments fleeting, gone so fast,
Yet the mirror, ever wise,
Keeps the secret in disguise.

Silent Sighs

Beneath the moon, where silence reigns,
Softly played in night's refrains,
Silent sighs and gentle dreams,
Flow like quiet, endless streams.

Stars above in silent glow,
Whisper words we'll never know,
In the stillness of the night,
All is calm, a tender sight.

Silent sighs, a lover's plea,
Bound in night's tranquility,
Echoes soft within the dark,
Gentle as a tiny spark.

Unspoken Cravings

In the hush of twilight's fall,
Longing whispers through the hall,
Unseen lips and quiet yearn,
In the shadows, secrets burn.

Hearts that beat with silent fire,
Unspoken cravings never tire,
Hidden deep and yet so near,
Bound by love and tethered fear.

Eyes convey what words betray,
Desires that won't fade away,
In the stillness, hear the call,
Unspoken cravings, after all.

Distant Affection

Across the miles, a heart does beat,
In rhythm with the marked retreat,
For distance, though it keeps apart,
Holds a tender, loving heart.

Whispers travel on the breeze,
Softly carried, meant to please,
Distant affection, yet so true,
Bridging gaps 'tween me and you.

When the stars adorn the sky,
And the moon is riding high,
Feel the warmth of love's embrace,
Distant, yet so full of grace.

Veiled Desires

In the moon's ethereal light,
Veil of dreams ignites the night.
Whispered wishes, soft as air,
Dance with shadows, unaware.

Fingers trace the starry sky,
Yearning for a love gone by.
Silent promises, unspoken,
Echoes of a heart once broken.

Hidden hopes in twilight's beam,
Fading like a distant dream.
Eyes that gleam with secret fire,
Guard the soul's veiled desire.

The Absent Reply

Letters penned in fading ink,
Words dissolve, and hopes do shrink.
Lonely wind through window sighs,
Whispers tales of absent replies.

Heartbeats lost in empty halls,
Echoes of the unanswered calls.
Memories that time would bind,
Seek the words they cannot find.

Candles flicker, shadows sway,
Ghosts of voices, swept away.
Silent tears in the moon's soft hue,
Yearn for answers never true.

Wordless Sorrows

Eyes that speak in silent tones,
Hold the sorrows no one owns.
Shattered dreams on lips that part,
Bleed the secrets of the heart.

Tears that fall like autumn leaves,
Whisper truths that no one heeds.
Breezes sigh and gently weep,
Cradle nights of wordless sleep.

Shadows linger, silent cries,
Reflect the pain in hollow eyes.
Grief's embrace, a soft caress,
In the realm of sorrows, wordless.

Wistful Nights

Stars that glimmer, soft and bright,
Guide the dreams of wistful night.
Moonlight whispers, tender breeze,
Sway the hearts and calm the seas.

Old regrets and futures vast,
Weave together, shadows cast.
In the silence, thoughts take flight,
Wander through the wistful night.

Soft the hours, sweet the air,
Wrap the soul in gentle care.
In this stillness, hearts align,
Bound by whispers, dreams entwine.

Echoes of a Solitary Heart

In the quiet corners of the night,
Where moonlight softens every scar,
A solitary heart takes flight,
Wandering where the echoes are.

Whispers of love long left astray,
Dances in shadows, lost in time,
Hoping dreams would come to stay,
In the rhythm of a silent rhyme.

Beneath the stars, so high above,
In solitude, it seeks embrace,
Echoes chant the tales of love,
In the heart, they leave their trace.

Chasing Shadows

Beneath the canopy of endless skies,
Where sun and shadow intertwine,
A fleeting dream of whispered lies,
Evaporates like morning wine.

In woodland paths where echoes stray,
Silent steps trace the unseen,
Beyond the reach of light's array,
Shadows dance, a ghostly sheen.

Through twilight's grasp, in twilight's hold,
The shadows hide, they come and go,
In the chase, we're young and old,
In their steps, the night will grow.

Empty Letters

Ink has faded, pages brittle,
Words that once meant all and more,
In empty letters, love is little,
Silent whispers on a shore.

Promises in written lines,
Between the spaces, voids remain,
They drift like long-forgotten vines,
Mourning under gentle rain.

Memories linger in the fold,
Where heart and pen did once confide,
Empty letters, growing cold,
A story lost on quiet tides.

The Waiting Silence

Between the breaths of midnight's air,
Where silence stretches far and wide,
In waiting there, beyond despair,
The quiet yearns to turn the tide.

In shadows cast by moon's embrace,
A stillness holds the world at bay,
It waits for dawn's soft, golden trace,
To chase the lingering dark away.

Through endless ages of the night,
The silence speaks in muted tones,
It waits for light to share its sight,
Where hope within the dusk is sewn.

Distant Heartbeats

In the quiet, moonlit night
Dreams and stars take flight
Whispers ride on silver streams
Chasing long-lost, distant dreams

Hearts once close now far apart
Timeless beats, an aching art
Memories tug on fragile strings
Lonely nights when silence sings

The wind carries tales untold
Of love and warmth, now grown cold
Each heartbeat, a distant call
Echoes in the night, one and all

Empty Echoes

Hollow sounds fill the air
Empty spaces, everywhere
Conversations without voice
Silent tears, a muted choice

Ghostly whispers haunt the hall
Shadows dancing on the wall
Each echo, a lingering pain
From fleeting moments that remain

Lonely rooms and vacant dreams
Life unraveling at the seams
Echoes of what used to be
Reverberate through memory

Fading Glances

Eyes that once were bright and clear
Fade with time, and disappear
Moments stolen by the past
Glimpses lost, too brief to last

Mirrored eyes reflect the pain
Of memories, like fleeting rain
Glances caught in twilight's glow
Slip away, before they grow

Silent stares across the way
Words unspoken fade to gray
Fading glances, fleeting light
Lost to time, and endless night

Lonely Whispers

Lonely whispers fill the night
Soft as shadows, out of sight
Carrying the weight of grief
Seeking solace, craving relief

Hidden voices lost in crowd
Yearning for a love avowed
Whispers travel through the air
Touching hearts in deep despair

In the dark, where dreams reside
Whispers seek a place to hide
Lonely souls and whispered pleas
Find their way among the trees

The Lonely Star

In the vast expanse of night,
One star glows with silent might,
Alone it whispers, calm and bright,
A beacon in the endless flight.

Through the void, its light persists,
A tender glow that never resists,
Guiding lost souls through cosmic mists,
On journeys long and unforeseen twists.

It stands apart, yet deeply feels,
The weight of night's celestial wheels,
A solitary gleam that heals,
A silent promise it reveals.

In darkness vast and cold afar,
Exists a solitary star,
Its mournful gaze, a tender scar,
Yet shines with hope, wherever you are.

Chasing Mirages

Across the desert's golden sand,
I chase a dream, so close at hand,
Yet every step reveals a strand,
A mirage fades, like shifting land.

The sun beats down, the air is dry,
Illusions glimmer, by and by,
In heat's embrace, where visions lie,
I seek the truth beneath the sky.

A fleeting shadow, fragile and frail,
I follow trails that twist and veil,
Through parched terrain and endless rail,
Each breath, a story, every gale.

In search of hope, I wander far,
Guided by an ephemeral star,
Though mirages deceive and mar,
Each step, a wish, a boundless scar.

The Void Within

Deep within where shadows play,
A void exists, both night and day,
Emptiness that seeks to sway,
The heart that yearns for a brighter way.

An abyss of thoughts, the mind concealed,
Whispers of fears, oft revealed,
In silence, wounds may be healed,
Yet void within remains, unsealed.

With every thought, a fleeting glance,
A dance within, a fractured chance,
To fill the void and find romance,
In life's enduring, silent trance.

Embrace the void, its darkness stark,
In seeking light, ignite a spark,
For even in the blackest dark,
A glimmer waits, a hopeful mark.

Echoes in the Wind

Voices carried on the breeze,
Whisper tales through swaying trees,
Echoes dance with subtle ease,
In nature's song, a soul finds peace.

From mountaintops to valleys low,
The winds of time forever blow,
With secrets that the ages know,
They tell of life's eternal flow.

Each whisper holds a story bright,
Of love and loss, of day and night,
In echoes soft, or wild in flight,
The wind's embrace, a pure delight.

On gentle wings, the past is shown,
In every gust, a memory known,
Through echoes in the wind, we're grown,
And with its song, we're never alone.

Dreams Unshared

In shadows deep, where visions stray,
A whispering night, whilst we delay,
Dreams unshared, like untold tales,
In silent hearts, where courage fails.

Stars above, they weave and dance,
In the cosmos, a fleeting glance,
Yet here we stand, our hopes concealed,
In whispered vows, they are revealed.

In the quiet, dreams take flight,
Bathed in soft, enchanting light,
Unspoken truths, in shadows cast,
Future's promise, tied to the past.

Eyes that meet but share no word,
Silent symphonies, unheard,
A promise kept beneath the moon,
Of change, and dreams, coming soon.

Yearnings deep within the soul,
In whispered breaths, they make us whole,
Dreams unshared, yet ever near,
In silent night, our hearts they steer.

Solitude's Companion

In the forest, where shadows blend,
Solitude becomes a friend,
Whispered winds in trees so tall,
A haunting, ancient, primal call.

By the river, soft and clear,
Lonely paths seem less severe,
Nature's whispers, softly sung,
Where silence speaks, with gentle tongue.

A cabin's light in twilight's fade,
In solitude, peace is made,
Echoes of the mind set free,
To wander wild, infinity.

Crisp leaves fall with autumn's breath,
In solitude, we meet our depths,
Inner worlds, through silence found,
Where lost spirits can unbound.

Alone, yet not in loneliness,
Solitude, a sweet caress,
In the quiet, hearts repair,
Solitude's Companion, always there.

Longing from Afar

Across the sea, where skies align,
Heartfelt pulses keep in time,
Whispers of a distant shore,
Longing hearts forevermore.

Letters written, stars to guide,
Silent tears that never hide,
Memories on misty breeze,
Longing thoughts with subtle ease.

Moonlit nights, a silvered dream,
Connected through an unseen beam,
From afar, our spirits touch,
Longing hearts that love so much.

Waves crash softly, secrets tell,
Of far-off lands where lovers dwell,
In the night, across the span,
A whisper of a loving plan.

Eyes that gaze beyond the sea,
Longing for what cannot be,
Yet in dreams, we're never far,
Eternal love, a guiding star.

Fading Glances

In twilight's shade, where shadows play,
Fading glances mark the day,
Moments lost in a lover's sight,
Drifting softly into night.

Eyes once bright, now dimmed and veiled,
Silent stories left unveiled,
In the fading of the light,
Lingered looks take flight.

Memories like fragile blooms,
In the dusk, the heart entombs,
Glances that once sparked a flame,
Fade away, too shy to claim.

Through the haze of twilight's grip,
Eyes release their loosened grip,
In the silence, tender glows,
Love's remnants softly flows.

Fading glances, whispers weak,
In the quietude, they speak,
Of moments fragile, yet so dear,
Fading, yet they linger here.

Flickering Hopes

Amid the twilight's gentle embrace,
A candle flickers soft and slow.
Dreams arise in the shadowed space,
Whispers of futures we wish to know.

Stars emerge in the velvet sky,
Each one a promise of what's to come.
Hope wavers but refuses to die,
In hearts where fear and faith are from.

The night's silence holds potent charms,
A dance of wishes on the air.
Though darkness may bring brief alarms,
A spark remains, bright and fair.

With dawn, the hopes flit and wane,
Yet, they leave an ember behind.
For in our hearts they shall remain,
A timeless guide for the blind.

So carry forth the flicker bright,
Through the shadows, flame alight.

Veiled Passion

In secret corners of the heart,
A flame burns quietly, unseen.
Two souls that fate could not part,
Entwined in a dance serene.

Eyes meet in moments hushed and rare,
A world within a fleeting gaze.
Passion's plea is whispered there,
In the abyss of lovers' maze.

The moon hides behind thickened cloud,
Yet, breathless whispers still confide.
Veiled passion speaks not aloud,
But in the silence hearts collide.

Desire wraps in shadows fine,
Leaving traces of what could be.
In hidden night, where stars align,
A love that's wild and free.

In quiet dreams, the secret's kept,
A token of the tears we've wept.

Unspoken Devotion

A glance across a crowded room,
A touch that lingers in the air.
Unspoken words that banish gloom,
A silent vow beyond compare.

No need for phrases, grand and bold,
For love is felt in heartbeats' hum.
In every gesture, tales unfold,
Of what we've shared and what's to come.

The world may turn and time may race,
Yet, in our gaze, a haven rests.
Unspoken devotion finds its place,
In moments time itself attests.

Beneath the mundane, love thrives,
A quiet strength, unseen but known.
In our hearts, it still survives,
A beacon when we're all alone.

So trust the silence and remain,
Forever bound, through joy and pain.

Chasing Phantoms

Through misty woods and shadowed glen,
We chase the dreams that dance away.
Phantoms of what might have been,
Haunt the light of breaking day.

Footfalls soft on dew-kissed ground,
Whispers echo through the trees.
In pursuit of what can't be found,
We seek the spectral memories.

Every shadow hides a tale,
Of moments lost and futures blurred.
With every step, doubts may assail,
Yet, hope in every heart is stirred.

Phantoms fade as dawn draws near,
Yet, their traces still remain.
Chasing dreams we hold most dear,
In every joy, in every pain.

For in the chase, we find our truth,
A dance of life, eternal youth.

Frozen Glimpses

In the icy realm of dreams,
Where time itself may cease,
Diamonds of frost gleam and scheme,
In a brittle, silent peace.

Frozen waters whisper low,
Secrets trapped beneath the ice,
Winds of winter softly blow,
Tales of life at winter's price.

Snowflakes dance in crystal skies,
Each unique yet cold and pale,
Like a mirror to the lies,
That are hidden in the gale.

Through the glass, the past is seen,
Moments caught in fragile frames,
Frozen glimpses stark and keen,
Echoes lost in wintry games.

Glimmer of a Smile

In the shadows of despair,
Where the heart is sore and wild,
Flickers once, elusive air,
The faintest glimmer of a smile.

Like a spark in endless night,
Drawing warmth where cold prevails,
Hope ignites, a soft delight,
Setting sail on tender gales.

Eyes that weep find strength anew,
In that brief, resplendent sheen,
Turning grey to vibrant hue,
With a grace so rarely seen.

Silent joy and whispered grace,
Mend the wounds of bitter trials,
Faint but sure, it leaves a trace,
In the glimmer of a smile.

Unseen Embrace

In the hush of twilight's grace,
When shadows tiptoe in the night,
There's an unseen, tender place,
Where spirits linger out of sight.

Silent whispers brush the air,
As if a ghostly hand does trace,
The lines of sorrow, light and fair,
In an unseen, gentle embrace.

Through the veils of mist and time,
Love persists beyond the eye,
Held in bonds pure, so sublime,
Embracing souls until they sigh.

In this realm, we're never lone,
Though unseen, love is near,
Embrace transcends the flesh and bone,
A silent, comforting veneer.

Silent Cries

In the stillness of the night,
Echoes reach the weary ear,
Silent cries from deepest plight,
Speak of sorrow, speak of fear.

Hidden beneath smiling faces,
Lies a world of untold pain,
In the crowded, empty spaces,
Silent cries pour down like rain.

Eyes that glisten with unshed tears,
Hold the secrets, never shown,
Yearning for a soul that hears,
Silent cries, to make them known.

In the silence, voices blend,
Calling out from depths profound,
Seeking solace, seeking friends,
In each silent, muffled sound.

The Empty Promise

A whisper on the fleeting breeze,
Promises made, now lost with ease.
Echoes of hopes that never came,
Left standing in the muted frame.

Stars above, they gently chide,
Of dreams once found, now brushed aside.
Moonlight casting shadows dim,
On vows that disappeared with him.

A heart that waits in silent pain,
For words once gold, now turned to chain.
Trust dissolved in night's cold mist,
Where empty promises persist.

In the dawn, the truth is clear,
No more deceit, no more to fear.
A new day breaks the dark facade,
Healing paths where hopes once trod.

Yet the scars, they softly gleam,
Reminding of each broken dream.
Lessons learned in sorrow's span,
Forging strength in heart of man.

Wandering Heart

Through the alleys, whispers call,
A heart adrift, seeking thrall.
In the maze of life's grand art,
Grows the tale of a wandering heart.

Mountains high and rivers deep,
Secrets held that shadows keep.
Journey carries, never part,
The quest within a wandering heart.

Stars above in midnight sky,
Guide the lost with open eye.
In the dark, a spark will start,
Igniting dreams of a wandering heart.

Voices past in winds align,
Echoes of a love divine.
Through the years, they play their part,
In the rhythm of a wandering heart.

Find the path where one belongs,
In the chorus of life's songs.
Still it beats, never to depart,
The enduring pulse of a wandering heart.

Frozen Petals

Petals touched by winter's chill,
Silent in the moonlight still.
Frozen in a fragile dance,
Whispers of a lost romance.

Snowflakes settle on their face,
Marking each a delicate grace.
In the frost, the past reveals,
Frozen petals, love congeals.

Memories in crystal light,
Hold the warmth of summer's night.
Time stands still as winter heals,
The frozen petals, hearts appeal.

In the thaw, as dawn does break,
Love again may re-awake.
Through the cold, a promise feels,
Frozen petals, life conceals.

Beauty held in winter's hand,
Silent as the frozen land.
Yet beneath, life's pulse appeals,
Frozen petals, hearts congeal.

Faded Footsteps

In the sand, where waves erase,
Faded footsteps leave no trace.
Silent echoes of the past,
Moments meant to never last.

On the path where shadows fall,
Memories etched on nature's wall.
Each imprint tells a story grand,
Of lives touched by fleeting hand.

Time will wash away the ground,
But whispers linger all around.
Faded footsteps, softly drawn,
Whisper tales of distant dawn.

In the hush of twilight's glow,
Softly does the memory flow.
Through the years, though faint they be,
Faded footsteps speak to me.

Though they vanish, leave no mark,
In our hearts, they set a spark.
Hidden trails through life's expanse,
Faded footsteps, nature's dance.

Silent Yearning

In shadows deep where secrets lie,
A silent yearning marks the still,
The echoes of a pleading sigh,
Through twilight's veil, they softly spill.

The heart concealed in muted grace,
With quiet hopes that swell and ache,
Beyond the stars, a silent place,
Where dreams unfold but never wake.

Mute whispers lace the midnight air,
A hidden song that angels weave,
While unseen hands through darkness dare,
To craft the dreams we all believe.

The world in hushed and silent bloom,
Speaks tales untold, in shadows born,
A longing grows within the gloom,
Where silent waves of thought are worn.

There lives a whisper, never known,
In silence deep, its story spun,
The unvoiced dreams, alone, have grown,
Until the rise of morning sun.

Moon's Unanswered Call

Through silver beams the moonlight flows,
A call unanswered, soft and clear,
It brightens dreams, yet where it goes,
Remains a secret to the ear.

The night doth hold its lonely play,
A serenade of cosmic love,
Where lunar ghosts in wistful sway,
Find solace in the stars above.

A hymn from ages long interlaced,
With echoes of the distant tides,
Yet earth below, in quiet haste,
Through slumbered journey gently glides.

Reflections on an ancient sea,
Where whispers of the moonlight fall,
Eternally entwined to be,
But ne'er to meet that distant call.

Within night's cradle, dreams embraced,
The silent cosmic voices stand,
For moon's unanswered call is traced,
Across the sky, by starlit hand.

One-Sided Whisper

In twilight shadows, secrets part,
A whisper from a distant space,
A single voice speaks to the heart,
Yet silence answers, void of grace.

The lonely words on quiet wing,
Cross endless nights, in search of ear,
They tell of sorrows, dreams they bring,
Through unseen tracks of time and fear.

Each whisper holds a latent hope,
A plea for echoes to return,
Yet in the dark, the heart must cope,
With fires unanswered, left to burn.

The stillness wraps its cold embrace,
Around the words that softly die,
As night winds trace their silent pace,
Across the bounds of moonlit sky.

A whisper, lone, without reply,
Through barren winds it finds its fate,
For love remains, though nights may fly,
In silent dreams to resonate.

Lonely Heartbeats

Within the night, where shadows creep,
A heartbeat sounds its lonely call,
In silent rooms where dreamers sleep,
It echoes off each empty wall.

A rhythm of a distant pain,
An ache that finds no place to rest,
It pulses in the midnight rain,
And lays its sorrowed plea to test.

No other heart responds in kind,
The beat continues all alone,
In solitude by fate designed,
Its cadence like a muted moan.

In every throb, a tale untold,
Of longing's depth and love unclaimed,
A symphony of feelings bold,
Yet all unknown, by night, untamed.

But still it beats through endless night,
In hopes another heart replies,
Till dawn's first light doth end its flight,
On whispered wings, it softly dies.

Overlooked Heartstrings

In the whisper of leaves,
Where shadows softly cling,
Lies the song of heartstrings,
That no one hears them sing.

Beneath the twilight's veil,
In twilight's gentle hold,
Whispers turn to tales,
Of love left untold.

The stars above that shine,
Reflect a secret glow,
Of dreams that intertwine,
In melodies they know.

Silent heart's devotion,
In moonlight's tender lace,
Overlooked emotion,
In a quiet, hidden place.

In the dawn so fleeting,
The sunrise paints the air,
Yet heartstrings keep on beating,
In a song only they dare.

Bittersweet Silence

In the hush of twilight,
Where silence finds its throne,
Rest the echoes of the night,
In solitude alone.

Amidst the silent whispers,
That linger in the breeze,
The heart finds a bittersweet,
Tenderness with ease.

The quiet talks of yesterdays,
In shadows softly cast,
Memories of olden days,
That eternally last.

Silent tears like morning dew,
Fall unseen in the light,
Where heartache feels a love so true,
In the silence of the night.

Bittersweet the silence,
Where dreams and sorrows meet,
In the melody of stillness,
The heart's rhythm beats.

Love in the Shadows

In the shadows soft and deep,
Where the twilight dims the day,
Lies a love that dreams to keep,
In a hidden, tender way.

Beneath the moon's quiet gaze,
Two hearts find their secret place,
Where love's gentle whispers raise,
In an unseen, warm embrace.

The darkness hides the fears,
Of a love both brave and shy,
Yet in night's silent tears,
Their bond will never die.

Beneath the stars' bright gleam,
Their shadows intertwine,
In a love that's like a dream,
Eternal and divine.

In the velvet midnight's care,
Love's truth begins to show,
In the shadows, hearts declare,
A love the world can't know.

Untouched Emotions

Beneath the surface calm,
Lie feelings deep and vast,
Untouched yet warm as balm,
In the heart's eternal cast.

The eyes may seem so still,
Yet within a storm resides,
An ocean of emotions,
Where true feelings do abide.

Silent like the sunrise,
That heralds dawn's embrace,
Untouched emotions rise,
To cast a softer grace.

Amid the quiet lulls,
Of peaceful nighttime air,
The heart's deep secrets pulse,
In a silence rare and fair.

Through days of muted song,
And nights of gentle dreams,
Untouched emotions long,
To flow like silent streams.

Unheard Symphony

In the quiet, notes softly play,
Strings of emotions woven tight,
A melody that's lost in day,
Resonates deeply in the night.

Whispers of the unseen art,
Flows through air like gentle stream,
Echoes touching every heart,
In the span of a fleeting dream.

Unheard voices, silent chords,
Compose the symphony so rare,
Truths that words could scarce afford,
Breathe in every whisper there.

Harmonies in silence sing,
Tales of love, of loss, of time,
Every shadow echoes ring,
In this symphony, sublime.

Listen close, the soul can hear,
Songs that lie 'neath waking thought,
A sacred tune, pure and clear,
In silence found, yet never sought.

Dreams in Silence

When the moon whispers to the night,
Dreams unfold in silent grace,
Stars above, a tender light,
Guide us to a heartfelt place.

Past the echoes of the day,
In realms where shadows gently fall,
Silent hopes, like clouds, delay,
To weave a dreamscape for us all.

In the stillness, softly tread,
Paths unseen by waking eyes,
Where the silent dreams are led,
By the whispers of the skies.

Every silent wish that flows,
Marks the night with a secret trace,
In the dreams that silence knows,
We find our hidden, sacred space.

In this tranquil, silent flight,
Where our deepest hopes take wing,
Dreams in silence birth the light,
Of the dawn that they'll soon bring.

Melancholy Breezes

Through the trees, a somber song,
Breezes whisper soft and low,
Tales of times now far and gone,
In a voice both sad and slow.

Leaves are rustling, tales they tell,
Of the summer's golden glow,
Now the autumn's quiet spell,
Brings a chill, and dreaming flow.

Melancholy winds that sigh,
Through the twilight's tender sheen,
As the amber leaves comply,
Falling softly, gold and green.

Memories in the breezes' dance,
Echoes of what used to be,
In their folds, a ghostly chance,
Of a past, now wild and free.

Beneath the sky so vast and blue,
Breezes speak in whispered beams,
Of the days we once knew,
And the hopes we held in dreams.

Silent Yearnings

In the silence of the night,
Heartfelt whispers find their way,
Yearnings in the soft starlight,
Barely there, yet there they stay.

Every secret, every sigh,
Held within the quiet air,
Longing dreams that gently lie,
Unrevealed, yet always there.

Hushed desires that seek no voice,
Flow like rivers through the mind,
In the stillness, they rejoice,
In the love they hope to find.

Silent pleas and hidden tears,
Glide beneath the moon's soft gleam,
In the silence of our fears,
Hope can weave its fragile dream.

In the quiet, hear the call,
Of the yearnings yet unseen,
Soft and tender, they enthrall,
In the heart's most silent dream.

Vanished Promises

In twilight's gentle, fading hue,
Dreams once bright have gone askew,
Whispers linger, promises fade,
As the light begins to shade.

Echoes of what once was true,
Now are ghosts of me and you,
Silent vows and broken chains,
Lingering through life's remains.

The morning breaks but cannot find,
The bond that once two hearts did bind,
Lost in shadows, hopes deferred,
In the quiet, not a word.

Time has swept away the trust,
Turning gold to endless dust,
Promises that once held sway,
Vanish in the light of day.

For as the stars in night's disguise,
Fade and vanish from our eyes,
So do dreams and promises,
Lost to life's contemptuous skies.

Hollow Embrace

In your arms, a chill I find,
A thousand miles, hearts not aligned,
The warmth we knew, an empty trace,
Time has left its hollow embrace.

Tender whispers, now just sighs,
Distant looks and faded eyes,
A love once whole, now out of place,
Lost within this hollow embrace.

Gone the laughter, soft and pure,
Memories less clear, unsure,
Silence now does interlace,
All the voids in hollow embrace.

Hands still touch, but not the soul,
Hearts apart, a fractured whole,
Spaces growing, time and space,
Deep within this hollow embrace.

Yet still we linger, shadows cast,
Holding on to moments past,
Hoping for the love we chase,
Escaping from this hollow embrace.

Echoes of Affection

In the quiet, echoes speak,
Of a love that time does seek,
Glimpses of affection's light,
Fleeting through the endless night.

Whispers of a sweet caress,
Tender moments we confess,
Fading echoes, love's reflection,
Lost within our own affections.

Memories like phantom grace,
Traces of a fond embrace,
Echoes linger, soft confession,
In the heart's concealed procession.

Nighttime holds the echoes dear,
Moments tender, all sincere,
Fading slowly, pure connection,
Echoes of our shared affection.

Time may steal the remnants there,
Shadows cast on love's affair,
Yet within, the heart's oblation,
Echoes holding true affection.

Shattered Daydreams

Once we soared in skies so blue,
Daydreams vivid, bright and true,
Life did change, those dreams unwind,
Leaving shattered hopes behind.

Glimmers of a future bright,
Lost within a deeper night,
Pieces fall and fade from view,
Shattered dreams of me and you.

Castles built in sand subdued,
Lost to tides and times unglued,
Daydreams felt by heart and mind,
Now just fragments left confined.

Every hope in morning's light,
Wilted in the fading sight,
Dreams once vibrant, now are dim,
Shattered by the world's own whims.

Yet in fragments, still may lie,
Glimmers of a past gone by,
Shattered daydreams may transform,
Into new hopes that keep us warm.

Unseen Desires

Beneath the veil of night's attire,
Lies a world of unseen desire.
Whispered dreams in silent fire,
Fuel the heart's unspoken choir.

Echoes dance in moonlit beams,
Painting shadows with elusive gleams.
Secrets held in midnight's schemes,
Intertwine in velvet dreams.

Unheard wishes gently glide,
Through the stillness, far and wide.
Longing souls that quietly bide,
In hidden realms where hopes abide.

Softly, softly, whispers call,
In the silence, rise and fall.
Unseen desires, one and all,
In the night, they stand tall.

Beneath the stars' celestial spire,
The heart's hidden fire,
Unseen desires never tire,
In the quiet, they aspire.

Quiet Longing

Upon the crest of dawn's first light,
Awakens quiet longing's plight.
Silent whispers through the night,
Yearning hearts, soft and slight.

The breeze that stirs the autumn leaves,
Carries with it subtle heaves.
Of wishes cast and heartfelt grieves,
In every gust, the soul believes.

Moonlit shadows on the wall,
Silent witnesses to the call.
Of dreams that rise and slowly fall,
In the quiet, standing tall.

The hush of twilight's gentle kiss,
Breathes of longing, whispered bliss.
In every sigh, a silent miss,
A quiet soul's soliloquy.

As stars adorn the evening sky,
Quiet longing passes by.
In tender murmurs, low and high,
It leaves a mark, though none know why.

Solitary Pulse

In echo's depth, where shadows play,
A solitary pulse holds sway.
Through silent night and muted day,
Its beat, relentless, stays at bay.

The heart alone in quiet thrall,
Listens to the yearning's call.
In solitude, it stands tall,
Against the void, it won't fall.

In whispered winds, it finds its rhyme,
Drawing breath from the sands of time.
A singular tune, low and prime,
Resonating, pure and fine.

Amidst the silence, strength does rise,
From unseen hopes, it meets the skies.
A solitary pulse defies,
The hollow echo of disguise.

Persistent beat within the chest,
A rhythmic song of unrest.
In each throb, longing is confessed,
The pulse endures, never suppressed.

Vanishing Warmth

In the twilight's dimming glow,
Vanishing warmth begins to show.
Fleeting moments, soft and slow,
Slip away as cool winds blow.

Echoes of a distant sun,
Fade as night's embrace is spun.
The day's warmth, its journey done,
In shadows deep, it comes undone.

Memory clings to fleeting heat,
In heart and soul, it finds retreat.
Though warmth may vanish, bittersweet,
Its essence lies in whispers fleet.

Stars emerge in cool night's hold,
Casting light, both soft and bold.
Vanishing warmth, a story told,
In twilight's arms, like tales of old.

In every dusk, an end does part,
Yet warmth remains within the heart.
Vanishing slowly at the start,
But ever-present in love's chart.

Blurred Lines of Love

In the haze of twilight's gleam,
Where whispers blend with dreams,
Two hearts in silent dance do meet,
Beneath the sky, so bittersweet.

Eyes that speak in muted tones,
Hands that sculpt with breath alone,
Love's boundary, blurred and worn,
A tender chaos newly born.

Fragmented light on faces drawn,
A tapestry of dusk till dawn,
Weaving threads both strong and weak,
In love's riddle, answers seek.

In every touch, a universe,
A secret shared, an unsaid verse,
Through shadows deep and light above,
Lives the art we call true love.

Harmony in discord found,
In every heartbeat's soft rebound,
As night unfolds her velvet glove,
So drift we through the lines of love.

Echoes in the Night

Whispers ride the midnight air,
Ghostly sighs that none can snare,
Through the silence, spirits creep,
Stirring dreams from restless sleep.

Moonlit paths and hidden fears,
Shadows trace forgotten tears,
Stars that pulse with ancient light,
Guide the echoes in the night.

Lonely calls from distant past,
Faint and fleeting, never fast,
Sounds of yore that haunt and cling,
Veil the night with unseen wings.

Listen, close your eyes and hear,
Sonic ghosts that hover near,
In the quiet, dark and deep,
Lies the song the night stars weep.

Mysteries in every tone,
Echoes of the night unknown,
Pierce the veil of shadowed light,
With melodies of endless night.

Silent Stars

Beneath a cloak of endless night,
Silent stars begin their flight,
Burning fierce in quiet grace,
Lighting up the vastest space.

Each a story brightly cast,
Echoes from a distant past,
Written in the twilight's scroll,
Secrets in the sky's control.

Silent watchers, still and true,
Glimmering in the inky blue,
Sentinels of cosmic lore,
Guardians of what's gone before.

As the world in slumber lies,
Silent stars adorn the skies,
Speaking words without a sound,
In the silence, truth is found.

Every shimmer tells a tale,
Of love and loss on epic scale,
In their silence, wisdom shines,
Stars that guard both space and time.

Shadows in the Moonlight

By the glow of silver beams,
Shadows dance in silent streams,
Waltzing through the night's embrace,
Painting secrets on the face.

Figures ghostly, thin, and long,
Whispering a phantom song,
Gather 'round the moonlit stage,
Actors in a dream's vague cage.

Moonlight weaves a haunting cloak,
Over hills and ancient oak,
In the stillness, shadows play,
Chasing night till break of day.

Softly tread where shadows drift,
Through the night with moon's pale gift,
In their silence, tales unfold,
Stories new and legends old.

Underneath the lunar glow,
Wandering where shadows flow,
In the dance of light and dark,
Hearts ignite with hidden spark.

Secret Embrace

Whispers in twilight's tender light,
Hearts convene in silent plight.
Veiled in dreams beyond night's lace,
We find solace in secret embrace.

Under stars that guard the night,
Our shadows dance, pure delight.
In the hush where moonbeams grace,
Undying love in secret embrace.

Through the stillness, time does weave,
Memories that bid us never leave.
Hidden paths we once did trace,
Journey bound in secret embrace.

Echoes of a world unseen,
Shared in glances, serene.
Promises no force could erase,
Cherished vows in secret embrace.

Dawning light might soon disperse,
Yet in hearts, verses rehearse.
Till the end we'll interlace,
Eternal bond of secret embrace.

Cloaked Yearnings

In shadows cast by twilight's veil,
Lie secrets only hearts can hail.
Beneath the cloak of nights unfurled,
Whispers yearn in another world.

Hidden hopes by starlight framed,
Silent desires that can't be named.
Through the darkness, they twirl,
Mysterious hopes in another world.

In the stillness of the night,
Our hidden longings take flight.
Floating through the starry swirl,
Unveiled dreams in another world.

Phantom feelings softly tread,
On paths we've left unsaid.
In silence deep, our souls unfurl,
Veiled love in another world.

Yet as morning starts to break,
And shadows from their dreams awake.
Memories in hearts will curl,
Yearning still for another world.

Luminous Shadows

Beneath the stars, a secret beams,
A whispered world of hidden dreams.
Where shadows dance in silent streams,
Luminous glow in quiet gleams.

Night's embrace, a canvas wide,
Dark and light in complement abide.
In moonlit shades, none can hide,
Luminous whispers side by side.

Every shadow paints a tale,
Where light and dark in balance sail.
Fleeting glows, like whispers frail,
Luminous shadows leave a trail.

Mysteries blend in twilight's hue,
Between the stars and morning's dew.
In every shadow, a truth anew,
Luminous moments softly grew.

Thus we wander in the night,
Guided by that gentle light.
Hand in hand, sight to sight,
In luminous shadows, we'll take flight.

Crimson Nightmares

In the silence of midnight's glare,
Fearsome dreams begin to bear.
Haunting shadows, whispers rare,
In the weave of crimson nightmares.

Moonlight casts an eerie sheen,
Echoes from a world unseen.
Fear's dark grasp, cold and keen,
Chilling depths of crimson dreams.

Whispers of despair take flight,
Through the boundless, bleak night.
In the shadows hides the fright,
Terrifying crimson sights.

Hearts race with fearful dread,
As nightmares loom inside the head.
Every fear and terror fed,
In the realm of crimson threads.

Yet the dawn will soon dispel,
The horrors of the midnight's spell.
Memories of that dark will quell,
Fading echoes, crimson's farewell.

Yearning in Silence

Beneath the moon's soft, silver glow,
I whisper words the stars don't know.
My heart, a quiet, seeking wave,
In silent seas, its secrets crave.

Each night, it heeds a distant call,
A voice unheard, yet felt by all.
With every breath, a silent prayer,
For dreams of love to find me there.

The winds may howl, the storms may rage,
But still, my heart remains a sage.
For in its silence, truth is found,
In whispered thoughts that go unbound.

Though shadows dance and shadows fall,
My soul persists, above it all.
For yearning, tethered to the night,
Holds onto hope, and grips it tight.

So here, beneath the stars' embrace,
In silent yearnings, find my place.
A dance of hearts, in quiet hue,
Where dreams of love may yet come true.

Hidden Flames

Beneath my ribs, a fire resides,
A hidden flame where passion hides.
Its embers glow with longing's light,
In shadows cast by endless night.

The world may see a tranquil face,
Concealing sparks in fervent chase.
But deep within, infernos burn,
And to this fire, my heart returns.

Each secret glance, each stolen kiss,
Ignites the blaze I can't dismiss.
A conflagration, veiled in song,
Where unspoken desires belong.

In every breath, the flickers rise,
A heat that no one can disguise.
Yet fear and doubt build walls so high,
To cage the fire from prying eyes.

But in the dark, it fiercely roars,
Consuming dreams behind closed doors.
For hidden flames will find their way,
To set the night ablaze with day.

Cloaked in Longing

Enveloped in a cloak of night,
I walk the path where dreams take flight.
With shadows cast in moonlit hue,
I seek the one my heart once knew.

Each step, a whisper in the wind,
Of love that shadows cannot dim.
Through veils of dark, I find my way,
To where our whispered secrets lay.

The night conceals what daylight shows,
In hidden streams, emotion flows.
A river deep beneath the calm,
Of silent cries and whispered psalm.

Within the gloom, I see your face,
A vision dressed in longing's lace.
Though shadows cloak where light once shone,
Still, I search for you alone.

For in this night, where dreams collide,
My heart finds solace, love beside.
And though the dawn may steal away,
Cloaked in longing, night will stay.

Dreams Deferred

In the quiet of the morning dew,
When dreams deferred still seem so new.
With each sunrise, hopes take flight,
Yet fade away with gathering night.

A future painted with golden hues,
Becomes a canvas of subdued blues.
For in each heart, a silent cry,
Of dreams deferred that pass us by.

Each step, a dance on time's thin line,
A search for what we left behind.
As moments drift like stars afar,
We grasp at light, but find the scar.

Yet still we dream, for dreams renew,
In every dawn's forgiving hue.
Though deferred, they do not die,
But rest in hope beneath the sky.

So with each day, we dare to try,
To chase the dreams that never die.
For in their shadow, lives the light,
Of dreams deferred but burning bright.

Shadowed Love

In twilight's embrace, two hearts unite
Whispers of love, hidden from sight
Secret shadows dance upon the wall
In darkness, their silent call

Beneath the moon's watchful gaze
A quiet love in the night's haze
No sun to reveal, no dawn to part
Just shadowed love, in stillness held at heart

The stars bear witness to their plight
Silent vows beneath the night
In shadows deep, their spirits find
A love that's pure, beyond the mind

No words need utterance, no sight
Just touch and feel in the quiet night
Their shadowed love, a boundless sea
Where time stands still, eternally

In every darkened corner, lies
Whispers of this love that never dies
Bound by shadows, free from light
Two hearts entwined, in endless night

Untouched Passion

A flame that burns, never to consume
Untouched passion in a secret room
Eyes that meet, but hands refrain
A silent storm, a distant rain

Veins pulse with a fire untamed
Yet, still the heart remains unclaimed
A yearning force, unseen, confined
A dance of souls, in shadows blind

Silent echoes, hearts that cry
A whispered touch, a muted sigh
A love so wild, yet held so tight
A thirst unquenched, day and night

In dreams, their bodies intertwine
A passion pure, beyond the line
Yet, as dawn breaks, the spell does fade
Untouched passion, in light's cascade

Such longing eyes, yet hands resist
A love that aches, a soul's twist
Bound by fate, yet hearts still beat
In silent love, they find their heat

The Silent Song

In the quiet dawn, a melody sings
A silent song on whispered wings
No words to shatter, no chords to bind
Yet in the silence, love we find

Each heartbeat, a note profound
In the rhythm of love, they're bound
No need for voice, nor spoken verse
In quietude, they traverse

The wind carries their soft refrain
In every rustle, joy and pain
A song of love, pure and strong
Unheard, yet it's played lifelong

Together they dance in silent grace
In love's embrace, they find their place
No need for sound, nor symphony
Their silent song, infinity

As stars align and night unfolds
Their silent song, a tale retold
In every glance, in every breath
A love that sings, beyond death

Yearning Pulse

Beneath the skin, a pulse does beat
A yearning cry, both soft and sweet
A call to love, a siren's wail
In each heartbeat, a longing tale

A life untouched, a heart unbound
In restless sleep, they're found
The scars of time, yet fresh and raw
In every beat, love's gentle law

Awake, aware, with senses keen
Yet still untouched, in dreams they've been
This yearning pulse, a silent scream
A stretch of night, a silver beam

In hushed moments, their hearts entwine
In dreams fulfilled, they find the sign
Yet in the waking world, they part
This yearning pulse, a restless heart

Each beat, a promise, unfulfilled
A love that waits, a soul's build
In every echo, time does cease
This yearning pulse, their hearts' release

Ephemeral Affections

In twilight whispers hearts do sigh,
Lost in moments passing by,
A fleeting touch, then softly gone,
The night descends as dreams move on.

Stars above in their silent grace,
Echoes of a tender trace,
Each breath a dance of time's caress,
Ephemeral loves, we dare confess.

Moonlight's kiss on fallen leaves,
Whispers secrets twilight weaves,
Silent promises that fade away,
Affections melt with dawn's first ray.

Yet in the heart, those whispers stay,
Timeless, though night turns to day,
Ephemeral, but forever bound,
In fleeting love, a truth is found.

Embrace the moment, let it soar,
For love that's held, holds evermore,
Ephemeral, yet deeply real,
In every fleeting touch, we heal.

Veiled Longing

Behind the mist, a heart does yearn,
For love's return, no more to burn,
In shadows deep, a quiet plea,
For whispers lost across the sea.

Eyes that meet, but never hold,
Stories of a truth untold,
A longing veiled in silent eyes,
Fearing love that fleeting flies.

Hands that reach, but touch the air,
In empty space, love's silent stare,
Dreams that weave a distant shore,
Of hearts that join forevermore.

Nighttime falls, and dreams arise,
Veiling longing's deep disguise,
In the quiet, hearts combine,
Longing's veil as dreams entwine.

Awake, the morning's soft embrace,
Veiled longing finds its resting place,
But in the heart, that silent plea,
Forever echoes, wild and free.

Caged Emotions

In iron bars, my feelings rest,
A heart that beats within my chest,
Silenced thoughts, no voice to lend,
Emotions caged until the end.

A whisper's scream, a tear's refrain,
In hidden corners bred from pain,
Beneath the surface, waves unseen,
Emotions caged, a silent dream.

Through the night, a storm does brews,
Of love unspoken, longing hues,
In chains of fear, held tight and neat,
Emotions caged, no chance to meet.

Within the darkness, light does glint,
A key to solace, love's imprint,
To set them free, a painful flight,
Emotions caged, crave morning light.

Awake, unchained, let freedom sing,
Emotional release, on hopeful wing,
No longer bound by silent fears,
Emotions freed, dry these tears.

Tears in the Wind

Through fields of gold, I wander far,
Chasing dreams like falling star,
Yet pained with each and every stride,
Tears in the wind, nowhere to hide.

A whispered name on zephyr's breath,
Echoes of a love's long death,
In every gust, a sorrowed tone,
Tears in the wind leave hearts alone.

Sunset's fire, yet cold within,
Heartbreak's legacy does begin,
Each tear a tale of lost embrace,
Caught in the wind, a fleeting trace.

With every breeze, a memory fled,
Of things unsaid, of love that's bled,
Yet hope remains in dawn's first light,
Tears in the wind find strength in flight.

So onward through the winds of change,
Beneath the sky's vast, endless range,
Tears in the wind, though sorrow's mark,
Guide us toward a brighter spark.

Withering Hopes

In the garden where dreams were sown,
Petals now lie brittle and dry.
The winds of fate have coldly blown,
And shadows cloak the endless sky.

Promises made under moonlit skies,
Now but whispers in the night.
Eyes that once sparked with fire,
Dim with lost, forgotten light.

Seasons change and leaves do fall,
Echoes of laughter fade away.
A silent mourning, a curdled call,
In the twilight of a waning day.

Once a bloom rich with desire,
A heart now close to decay.
The ember of hope's dying fire,
Whispers of dreams in disarray.

Yet beneath the ice and the pain,
A seed of hope lies still.
For life must ebb to rise again,
Beyond the shadows of this hill.

Fading Love Songs

Melodies once vibrant and clear,
Now dissolve in the misty air.
Ballads sung with heartfelt cheer,
    Echo now, but nowhere.

Strings that once played in harmony,
Now out of tune, they ache and cry.
The notes of love, lost in cacophony,
    Beneath the somber sky.

Lips that whispered songs of grace,
    Now in silence, cold and tight.
Memories of a warm embrace,
    Fade into the endless night.

Journeys carved in the starlit tales,
Now but scars in shadowed dreams.
The ballad's end in whispered wails,
    Soft as moon's pale beams.

Yet listen close, and you may hear,
A tune reborn, from tear-streaked past.
For love's song, though faint and sheer,
    In hearts will forever last.

Invisible Wounds

In the quiet of the sleepless night,
Unseen sorrows lie in wait.
Whispers of a silent fight,
Beneath a smile, delicate and feint.

Scars that mar the unseen soul,
Hidden deep, and often brushed away.
Wounds that make the spirit whole,
Yet silently, they betray.

Eyes that shimmer with hidden pain,
Tears unshed, like dew in morn.
A struggle hard to ever explain,
A heart that's weary, worn.

The solace found in shadows deep,
Where light dares not pierce through.
In silence, secrets meet and seep,
Invisible wounds, old and new.

Yet, in the dark, a strength does rise,
From wounds unseen, to skies unknown.
For healing doesn't need our eyes,
But love, to call it home.

Evanescent Love

A fleeting touch, a whispered plea,
In the dusk, where shadows mend.
The ghost of love, a memory,
In twilight haze, it wends.

Eyes that shimmered with the dawn,
Now reflect a starless sky.
Moments grasped, like strands undone,
In the blink of a lover's sigh.

Time a thief, with merciless creed,
Steals the warmth of lovers' hold.
Hearts once fervent, now they bleed,
In the aching cold.

Promises like morning dew,
Gone before the rising sun.
In the dance of time, love, too,
Fades before it's even begun.

Yet in each ephemeral phase,
Lies a truth both soft and bright.
For love, though brief as twilight's gaze,
Is eternal in its light.

Milton Keynes UK
Ingram Content Group UK Ltd.
UKHW021835040724
444921UK00005B/62

9 789916 860847